Words Their Way™

Word Sorts for Letter Name— Alphabetic Spellers

Second Edition

Francine Johnston
University of North Carolina, Greensboro

Donald R. Bear
University of Nevada, Reno

Marcia Invernizzi
University of Virginia

Shane Templeton
University of Nevada, Reno

Allyn & Bacon
is an imprint of

PEARSON

Boston   New York   San Francisco
Mexico City   Montreal   Toronto   London   Madrid   Munich   Paris
Hong Kong   Singapore   Tokyo   Cape Town   Sydney

Vice President and Executive Publisher: Jeffery W. Johnston
Senior Editor: Linda Ashe Bishop
Senior Development Editor: Hope Madden
Senior Managing Editor: Pamela D. Bennett
Senior Project Manager: Mary M. Irvin
Editorial Assistant: Demetrius Hall
Senior Art Director: Diane C. Lorenzo
Cover Design: Ali Mohrman
Cover Image: Hope Madden
Operations Specialist: Matthew Ottenweller
Director of Marketing: Quinn Perkson
Marketing Manager: Krista Clark
Marketing Coordinator: Brian Mounts

For related titles and support materials, visit our online catalog at www.pearsonhighered.com

Library of Congress Cataloging-in-Publication Data

Words their way : word sorts for letter name-alphabetic spellers / Francine Johnston . . . [et al.].—2nd ed.
   p.cm.
  Includes bibliographical references.
  ISBN–13: 978-0-13-514580-7
1. Word recognition 2. English language—Orthography and spelling I. Johnston, Francine R.
LB1050.44.W68 2009
372.63'2—dc22

                                                        2008002484

14 13 12

Allyn & Bacon
is an imprint of

Contents

Overview

Word Sorts for Letter Name–Alphabetic Spellers is a companion volume to the core text Words Their Way: Word Study for Phonics, Vocabulary, and Spelling Instruction (WTW). The core text supplies the theory and research that underlie the curriculum laid out in these companions and it is important that teachers have this text available for reference. This collection of sorts includes both pictures and words for students who are in the letter name–alphabetic stage of spelling. Chapter 5 in WTW describes this stage in detail. Letter name–alphabetic spellers are usually in late kindergarten and first grade and should know how to hear and spell most consonant sounds in preparation for the features in this book. To figure out exactly where individual students should start within this supplement, you need to administer one of the spelling inventories and use the feature guides in Chapter 2 of WTW.

SCOPE AND SEQUENCE OF THIS BOOK

A quick review of initial consonants is provided first in five lessons. Same-vowel word families are then introduced with words and pictures and then digraphs and blends are covered using picture sorts. Word families are revisited in mixed-vowel contrasts and include words with digraphs and blends. Students then focus on the short vowel itself in sorts that move beyond families and continue to review digraphs and blends in CVC words. Finally there is a brief introduction to r-influenced vowels compared to short vowels and a simple contraction sort.

RESOURCES

For each unit, Notes for the Teacher provides placement guidelines and background information about the features of study. The notes also describe weekly routines that ensure practice and enrichment and offer suggestions for literature connections and games. For each lesson there are directions for how to introduce the sort as well as additional teaching tips. Sorts are presented as black line masters that can be reproduced so that each student can sort their words a number of times. We recommend that you enlarge the sorts about 10% to maximize the paper size. You should also use the masters to prepare a set of pictures and words for modeling. You may want to make a transparency of the sort and cut it apart for use on an overhead or enlarge the words for use in a pocket chart. You can also simply make your own copy to cut apart and use on a desktop or on the floor. See WTW and the accompanying CD-ROM for additional background information, organizational tips, games, and activities. Words Their Way for English Language Learners provides information to help you work with students who are not native speakers of English.

PLACEMENT AND PACING

This book contains eight units of study that are grouped by early, middle, and late designations in the table of contents. Following are general guidelines for placing students using the inventory results.

Early letter name–alphabetic spellers will know most of their letter sound correspondences for consonants but may still confuse *y* and *w*, *b* and *p*, or other similarly articulated consonants. Vowels will be used rarely. They will earn some points (5 to 6) on the Primary Spelling Inventory (in Chapter 2 of *WTW* under initial and final consonants but will not spell any words correctly. They will benefit from a review of initial consonants and then move into the study of same-vowel word families using picture support. If students are still missing three or more initial consonants they will need more work on consonants as described in *Word Sorts for Emergent Spellers*.

Middle letter name–alphabetic spellers will know initial and final consonants (earning 6 or 7 points in both categories on the Primary Spelling Inventory) and will also be using but confusing some medial short vowels (scoring 0 to 2 points for short vowels). They will earn few, if any, points for blends and digraphs. They are ready to study blends and digraphs with pictures and mixed-vowel word families.

Late letter name–alphabetic spellers will spell some short vowels correctly (earning 2 to 4 points in that category) as well as many blends and digraphs (earning at least 4 to 7 points on those features). Sorts 38 to 47 focus on short vowels and offer some review of blends and digraphs. If students are spelling most short vowels (5 to 6) correctly AND most blends and digraphs (5 to 7) AND are using but confusing long-vowel markers, then they are ready to begin the study of long vowels in *Word Sorts for Within Word Pattern Spellers*. In the early sorts short vowels will be reviewed and compared to long vowels.

There are seven spell checks that can be used as pretests to gather more in-depth information about features and to place your students more accurately. For example, you might give Spell Check 2 (page 28) to assess students' knowledge of word families. If students spell 90% on a spell check correctly then you can safely move on to the next feature. Scores from 50% to 75% indicate an instructional level.

The pacing for these sorts is designed for slow to average growth. After introducing a sort you should spend 3 to 5 days following routines that encourage students to practice for mastery. However, if your students seem to be catching on quickly you can speed up the pace by spending fewer days on a sort or you may skip some sorts altogether. However, you may need to slow down and perhaps even create additional sorts for some students using pictures from *WTW* and word lists throughout this book and in *WTW*. Templates to create these additional sorts can be found in *WTW* and at the end of this book.

ENGLISH LANGUAGE LEARNERS

Words Their Way for English Language Learners provides information to help you work with students who are not native speakers of English. If students are literate in their first language they may try to spell the sounds they hear in English with the correspondences they know from their first language. Word sorting lessons will help them sort out the differences and focus their attention on new sounds and patterns but expect ELL's to need extra practice and support. Here are several suggestions.

1. Reduce the number of words in a sort.
2. Spend more time saying the words aloud and discussing meanings, not just in the introductory lesson, but throughout the week.
3. Pair ELLs with English speakers for partner work.
4. Accept variations in pronunciation (even native English speakers pronounce vowel sounds in a variety of ways) and allow students to sort in ways that make sense to them but still reflect sound and pattern correspondences.

Unit I Review Sorts for Initial Consonants

NOTES FOR THE TEACHER

Targeted Learners

These five picture sorts are designed to quickly review the initial consonants. Such a review may be especially useful for first graders at the beginning of the year and for all students in the early letter name stage. If students have missed only one or two consonants on a spelling inventory and you see that they are representing most consonants correctly in their writing, then a fast-paced review, doing a new sort every 2 to 3 days, may be all that is needed. Students who are still confusing many initial consonants probably need a slower pace, spending a week on each sort. You may want to use Spell Check 1 on page 12 for a pretest to see which children really need such a review and which consonants need to be reviewed. Additional review will take place as students work with same-vowel word families in the next unit.

Teaching Tips

Students in the letter name–alphabetic stage may confuse letter sound matches because the name of the letter suggests a different sound. This is true for *y* ("wie") whose name begins with a/w/sound, *g* ("jee") which begins with /j/, and *h* ("aich") which does not have the /h/ sound but ends with /ch/. Other confusions arise over sounds that are articulated similarly: *p/b, t/d, f/v, g/k*. In addition, English Language Learners will have confusions based on their language (see *WTW* and *WTW* for ELLs for specific information). For students who exhibit these confusions you might want to prepare some sorts that contrast the very letters or sounds they are confusing. *WTW* provides pictures and a template to use for this purpose. For example, you might prepare a sort with pictures that begin with *y* and *w*.

Most students learn the letter sound matches for final consonants along with initial consonants and work with same-vowel word families helps to focus attention on final consonants. Once students develop the phonemic awareness to isolate and attend to final consonant sounds, the matches come easily. However, students who lack this phonemic awareness or students whose native language does not have many final consonant sounds, as in Spanish, may need extra work with final consonants. Look for pictures in the Appendix of *WTW* and use a blank template such as the one at the end of this book to prepare final consonant picture sorts.

Standard Routines for Use with Picture Sorts

1. *Repeated Work with the Pictures.* Students should repeat the sort several times after it has been modeled and discussed under the teacher's direction. Make a copy of the black line master for each student, enlarging it to reduce paper waste and

Literature Connection

Share a book such as *Miss Bindergarten Gets Ready for Kindergarten* (by Joseph Slate and Ashley Wolff) and revisit it as each group of initial sounds is reviewed to find the names of Miss Bindergarten's students and other words associated with each letter. Keep lots of alphabet books handy for word searching. *Animalia* (by Graeme Base) is a puzzle book especially fun to search for words that begin with each letter of the alphabet. Students will find "lazy lions lounging at the library" along with many more *l* words hidden away in the two-page illustration.

increase the size. After cutting out the pictures and using them for individual practice, the pieces can be stored in an envelope or plastic bag to sort again several times on other days. See *WTW* for tips on managing picture sorting.

2. *Draw and Label and Cut and Paste.*   For seat work, students can draw and label pictures of things that begin with the target sounds/letters. They can also look for pictures in magazines and catalogs and paste those into categories by beginning sound. The pictures from the black line sort also can be pasted into categories and children can then label the pictures. This can serve as an assessment tool but *do not* expect accurate spelling of the entire word at this time.

3. *Word Hunts and Word Banks.*   Students can look through their reading materials and word banks for words that have the targeted consonant sounds and record these. Alphabet books are also a good place to look for additional words that begin with targeted sounds. Plan a time for sharing their findings.

4. *Games and Other Activities.*   Many games are described in *WTW* and are available to print out from the *WTW* CD-ROM. Variations of the Follow the Path game work especially well with beginning sounds.

SORTS 1–5   BEGINNING CONSONANT SOUNDS

(See page 7.) Because all of the sorts work very much the same way, we provide only one set of directions. Use Sort 1 as an example.

Demonstrate, Sort, Check, and Reflect

1. Prepare a set of pictures to use for teacher-directed modeling. Use the letter cards as headers and display the pictures randomly with picture side up. Name the pictures with your students, especially if you have any English Language Learners.
2. Begin a **sound sort** by introducing the headers: BELL *begins with /b/ and is spelled with the letter* b. Then model how to sort one word into each column explaining explicitly what you are doing: *Here is a picture of a bug.* Bug *starts with the /b/ sound made by the letter* b *so I will put it under the picture of the bell. This is a picture of a map.* Mmmmap *starts with the /m/ sound made by the letter* m *so I will put it under the picture of the mouse.* Model a picture under *r* and *s* in the same manner and then say: *Now who can help me sort the rest of these pictures?* Continue with the children's help to sort all of the pictures. Ask them to name the picture and name the letter it goes under: Roof *begins with r.* Let mistakes go for now. Your sort will look something like the one shown in Figure 1.
3. When all the pictures have been sorted, name them in columns and check for any that need to be changed: *Do all of these sound alike at the beginning? Do we need to move any?*

Figure 1

4. Repeat the sort with the group again. Keep the letter cards as headers. You may want to mix up the words and turn them face down in a deck this time and let children take turns drawing a card, naming it, and sorting it in the correct column. You can also simply pass out the pictures and have the children take turns sorting them. After sorting, model how to check by naming the words in each column and then talk about how the words in each column are alike.

Extend

Give each student a copy of the sort for individual practice. Assign them the task of cutting out the pictures to sort on their own in the same way they did in the group. Give each student a plastic bag or envelope to store the pieces. On subsequent days students should repeat the sorting activity several times. Involve the students in the other weekly routines listed on pages 3–4 and described in *WTW* for the letter name–alphabetic stage.

Sort 2 Beginning Consonants *t, g, n, p*

Tt tent	*Gg* ghost	*Nn* net	*Pp* pig
towel	gate	needle	pen
tub	gum	nut	pipe
tire	gas	newspaper	pail
tie	goose	nose	pan
two	goat	nails	pin

Sort 3 Beginning Consonants *c, h, f, d*

Cc cat	*Hh* hand	*Ff* fish	*Dd* dog
corn	horn	fork	dice
can	hook	fox	deer
cane	hose	four	desk
cow	horse	fence	dive
candle	house	fan	dishes

Sort 4 Beginning Consonants *l, k, j, w*

Ll lamp	*Kk* key	*Jj* jug	*Ww* watch
lips	kitchen	jeep	well
log	kangaroo	jacks	worm
leg	kitten	jump	wing
leaf	kick	jacket	window
lock	kite	jar	witch

Sort 5 Beginning Consonants *y, z, v*

Yy yarn		*Zz* zipper		*Vv* van	
yoyo	yarn	zebra	zipper	vest	vine
yogurt	yard	zoo		vase	violin
yawn	yell	zigzag		vacuum	volcano
yolk		zero		van	

SPELL CHECK 1   ASSESSMENT FOR BEGINNING CONSONANTS

All the consonants are assessed with Spell Check 1 on page 12. This is designed for use as either a pretest or a posttest. To administer the assessment, name each picture and encourage children to spell as much of the word as they can, even though they will only be formally assessed on the initial sounds. If students are representing some of the vowels and many final consonants, then they should be ready for the study of word families. The pictures are:

1. lips	**2.** top	**3.** mat	**4.** kite
5. duck	**6.** bat	**7.** yell	**8.** game
9. rope	**10.** net	**11.** jet	**12.** zipper
13. foot	**14.** pig	**15.** soap	**16.** web
17. vine	**18.** cup	**19.** ham	

SORT 1   Beginning Consonants *b*, *m*, *r*, *s*

Bb	Mm	Rr	Ss

SORT 2   Beginning Consonants *t, g, n, p*

Tt	Gg	Nn	Pp

SORT 3   Beginning Consonants *c, h, f, d*

Cc	Hh	Ff	Dd

SORT 4   Beginning Consonants *l, k, j, w*

Ll	Kk	Jj	Ww

SORT 5   Beginning Consonants y, z, v

Yy	Zz	Vv	

Spell Check 1   Assessment for Beginning Consonants

Name _____

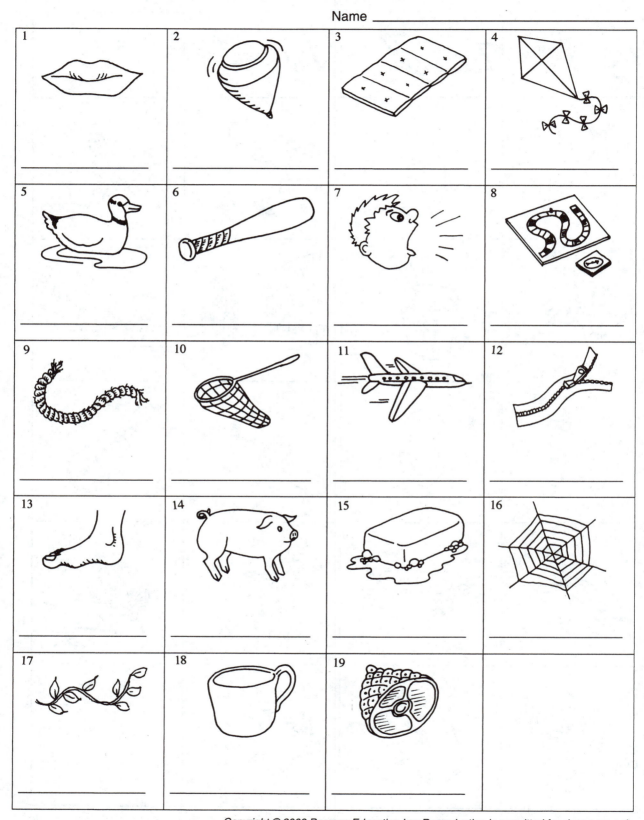

Unit II   Same-Vowel Word Families with Pictures

NOTES FOR THE TEACHER

Background and Objectives

Word families or phonograms that share the same vowel are a good way to review consonants and introduce students to short vowels and the visual aspects of rhyme. While working with word families, children will practice phonological blending skills as they learn to say the **onset,** or first sound (such as the *c* in *cat* or the *fl* in *flat*), and add on the **rime** (the vowel and what follows such as the *at* in *cat*) to figure out a word. Asking students to isolate or blend the onset and rime (*c-at*) is easier than asking them to isolate or blend individual phonemes (*c-a-t*). Sorts that isolate and contrast the vowels will come later and then students will be taught to discriminate and identify the short vowel. This unit introduces same-vowel word families with the support of pictures. A later unit of mixed-vowel word families repeats many of these same families but without the picture support. Students will:

- Sort pictures and words by rhyming sound and identify rhyming words
- Match words to pictures using beginning and ending consonant sounds
- Learn to isolate, identify, and blend the onsets and rimes in word families
- Read and spell words in families that contain the same short vowel

Targeted Learners

These sorts can be used with early letter name spellers who have mastered consonants in the initial positions and are using some consonants in the final positions (spelling *fun* as FN or *wet* as WT). They may be including some medial vowels (as in BOT for *boat*). Typically these children are in late kindergarten and early first grade. Initial and final consonants will be reviewed in these sorts, and blends and digraphs will be introduced. Spell Check 2 on page 28 can be used as a pretest and posttest. Students who score at least 90% can move on to other features.

Teaching Tips

The seven sorts in this unit feature words and pictures and focus on only one vowel at a time. In general, spend several days with each sort, implementing the routines described below. We especially recommend building, blending, and extending. To slow the pace, spend more time on each sort or focus on only one family at a time before comparing two families. Different pacing scales are suggested in *WTW*.

ELLs whose native language does not have a lot of final consonants or rhyming words may have some difficulty initially with these sorts, but they offer good practice for saying and hearing final consonant sounds and the pictures provide added support.

Literature Connection

When possible, share books that contain a number of words from the target families as a way to introduce or reinforce the families. For example, *Cat on the Mat* by Brian Wildsmith is a natural connection with the *at* family and *Dan the Flying Man* published by the Wright Group has a number of words in the *an* familiy. *Hop on Pop* by Dr. Seuss features a variety of families. Many publishers have prepared little books written on an appropriate beginning reading level that feature words families such as Ready Readers by Pearson Learning Group. Websites also offer little books that can be printed out and used. Those at Hubbard's Cupboard are free. These little books are not great literature but do serve to reinforce the targeted features.

You may also have jingles and rhymes that feature two or more words in a family such as the ones listed below. You can present these on a chart or overhead and underline target words before or after doing the sorting and activities. Copies of nursery rhymes and other materials related to word families are available at a number of websites. One favorite is Rhyme-A-Week created by Laura Smolkin at http://curry.edschool.virginia.edu/go/wil/rimes_and_rhymes.htm. Here are a few examples:

Old Mother Hubbard: *at* (*cat, hat*) and *ig* (*wig, jig*)
Jack and Jill: *ill* (*Jill, hill*)
Five Little Speckled Frogs: *og* (*frog, log*)
To Market, To Market: *ig* (*pig, jig*) and *og* (*hog, jog*)

Standard Routines for Use with Word Families

1. *Repeated Work with the Pictures and Words.*   Students should work with the featured sorts several times after the sort has been modeled and discussed as described in each following lesson. After cutting out the words and pictures and using them for individual practice, students can store the pieces in an envelope or plastic bag to sort again several times on other days. The pictures and words can also be used in partner activities during which children work together to read and spell the words. At some point, children may glue the sort onto paper or keep it to combine with additional sorts in review lessons.

2. *Building, Blending, and Extending.*   Students should be able to read and spell these words, so work is required on both. See the letter cards on page 106 to use for building, blending, and extending with the onsets and rimes on separate cards. These can be enlarged for use in a pocket chart and can also be duplicated (after enlarging) for use by individual students. Magnetic letters also work well but keep the rime unit together when working with word families.

   For **building,** say the word and then model how to make the word by putting together the onset and then the rime as shown in Figure 2. Model how to change the onset to create other words familiar from the sort. Children can work with similar materials at their places using their own letter cards or a Show Me folder (described in *WTW* and available for printing from the CD-ROM).

   For **blending,** place the onset and rime in a pocket chart or write them on the board. Say the onset and then the rime as slowly as possible without distortion (e.g., /ssss/ pause /aaaat/) pointing to the *s* and then the *at* as a unit. Then say the word naturally as you run your hand under it or push the cards together: *sat*. Model how you can change the onset to create a new word such as *mat*. Have the students

Figure 2

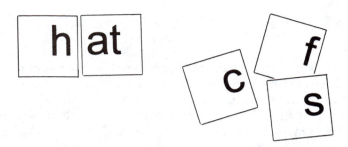

say the sounds with you and then individually. Do not isolate the vowel and the final sound. Children should learn these as a unit at this point.

For **extending,** include words in the blending activity from the list of additional words in each lesson. This will help students see that knowing a word family can help them figure out many additional words as well as the ones featured in the sort. Be aware that words with blends and digraphs will pose special challenges if students have not yet studied these features. Only a few words with blends and digraphs are included in Sorts 6 to 12, but more can be introduced in a group activity when the teacher can support students' efforts. This is an important way to foreshadow the work on digraphs and blends that will come next.

3. *Reading.*   Use decodable texts or little books that have a number of words with the featured family. Many publishers are now creating "phonics readers," and some of them focus on word families. Be sure students can read these books with 90% accuracy on a second reading.

4. *Word Recognition.*   After students have worked with the words and pictures for several days, hold up just the words and practice word recognition. Students can work in pairs to practice saying the words. Model blending of the onset and rime if students have trouble.

5. *Spelling.*   Hold up pictures one at a time and have the students spell the word using letter cards, chalk boards, white boards, or pencil and paper. Ask students to underline the letters (such as *at*) that are the same in every word. Students can also work with a partner, taking turns calling a word for their partner to spell and then showing the word to check it.

6. *Word Hunts.*   Look for words in daily reading that mirror the featured word families. Challenge children to find others that could go in the family or brainstorm additional words but understand that it may be difficult to find them. You may want to create posters or displays of all the words students can discover for each family.

7. *Games and Other Activities.*   Create flip books, letter slides, or word family wheels like those described in *WTW* and are ready to print from the *WTW* CD-ROM. The Show Me game is a word-building activity we highly recommend for use with all word families. Other games such as Word Maker, Roll the Dice, and Go Fish are described in Chapter 5 of *WTW*.

8. *Assessment.*   To assess student's weekly mastery, ask them to spell and read the words. Students can be given a traditional spelling test because they are now expected to spell the complete word. Have them number their paper and call aloud a sample of words from the lesson. A final spell check for the unit follows the collection of sorts and can serve as a posttest.

SORT 6   *AT* FAMILY WITH WORDS AND PICTURES

Demonstrate, Sort, Check, and Reflect

(See page 21.)

1. Prepare a set of pictures and words to use for teacher-directed modeling. Introduce the sort with a **matching activity.** Arrange the pictures in a column beginning with the most familiar words such as *cat* or *hat*. Have the students join in as you name them from top to bottom. Ask the students how those words are alike. If no one mentions that they rhyme you should supply that term: *These words* **rhyme.** Then arrange the word cards randomly below or off to the side where everyone can see them. Name the first picture and ask: *Can someone find the word* cat? *How did you know that word was* cat? *Yes it starts with a* c. Follow this procedure until all the words are matched to a picture as shown in Figure 3.

2. Read down the list of words and ask how they are alike. The idea that they rhyme should be restated as well as the idea that they all end in an *a* and a *t*. Introduce the idea that these words make up a **word family** because they all end with the same group of letters. They all end with *a-t*.

3. Remove the pictures. Arrange them randomly or hand them out to children in the group to match back to the words. Encourage children to tell how they could do the matching and once more ask how the words are alike.

Extend

Give each student a copy of the sort for individual practice and assign the students the task of cutting out the pictures and words to match them on their own in the same way they did in the group. Have them store their pieces in an envelope or plastic bag. On subsequent days, students should repeat the matching activity several times.

Figure 3

See the list of standard weekly routines for follow-up activities to the basic sorting lesson. Introduce building, blending, and extending as described under routines. The alternative words below for each sort can be used for the extending part, or that part can be skipped because there are not many additional words without involving blends and digraphs.

Additional Words.   *vat, brat, flat, scat, chat, that*

SORT 7   *AN* AND *AD* FAMILIES WITH WORDS AND PICTURES

Demonstrate, Sort, Check, and Reflect

(See page 22.) Prepare a set of pictures and words to use for teacher-directed modeling.

1. Introduce the pictures with a **rhyming sort.** Place the picture of the *can* and the *dad* as headers for the sort (see Figure 4). Explain that the students need to listen for rhyming words and put them under the correct picture. Select another picture such as *van*. Ask: *Does* van *rhyme with* can *or* dad? *Yes, it rhymes with* can *so we will put it under the picture of the can.* Continue until all the pictures have been sorted. Have the students join in as you name them from top to bottom. Ask the students how the words in each column are alike: *These words **rhyme.*** Leave the headers and remove the other pictures. Hand out the pictures or place them randomly to the side or in a deck. Call on children individually to help sort the words again by rhyme.
2. Next introduce the word cards. Arrange them randomly below or off to the side where everyone can see them. Name the first picture and ask if someone can find that word: *Can someone find the word* can? *How did you know that word was* can? *Yes it*

Figure 4

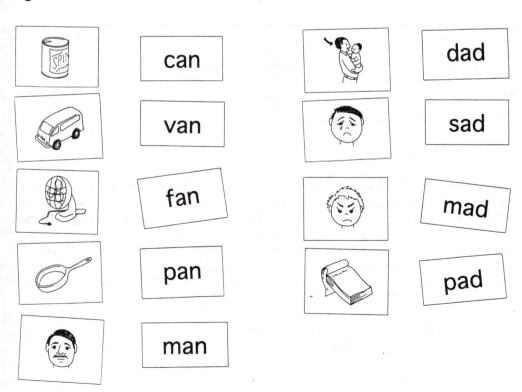

starts with a c *and ends with an* n. Follow this procedure until all the words are matched to a picture. Read down the list of words in one column at a time and ask how they are alike. Children should note that they rhyme and they end in the same two letters. Remind the students that they studied the *at* family and now they are studying two more families, the *an* and *ad* families.

3. Remove the words. Arrange them randomly, put them in a deck, or hand them out to children in the group to match back to the words. Encourage children to tell how they could do the matching and once more ask how the words are alike.

Extend

Make a copy of the sort for each child. See the list of standard weekly routines. In addition you can include some **review** using all three families (*at, an, ad*) from Sorts 1 and 2. Put out all the picture and words in a pocket chart or center and challenge students to sort into three categories. The words listed below can be used during building, blending, and extending.

Additional Words.   *ban, Dan, tan, plan, scan, that, bad, had, lad, Brad, glad, Chad*

SORT 8   AP AND AG FAMILIES WITH WORDS AND PICTURES

Demonstrate, Sort, Check, and Reflect

(See page 23.) Introduce the pictures with a rhyming sort as described for Sort 7. Good headers for this sort might be *cap* and *bag*. Always be sure to ask the students how the words in each column are alike and why they are called word families.

ap words and pictures		*ag* words and pictures	
cap	nap	bag	tag
lap		flag	wag
map		rag	

Extend

At this point you can **review** all five *a* families (*at, an, ad, ap, ag*) using pictures and words from Sorts 1, 2, and 3. Challenge students to sort into five categories. You might try this with just the words by creating your own word sort sheet. List words from all five families randomly for students to cut apart and sort by families. Follow this up with partner sorts where children take turns reading the words for their partner to sort. If you have not tried the Show Me game this is a good time to use it to review all five families. As you call out words for students to spell, the vowel will stay the same but the beginning and ending letters will change.

Additional Words.   *gap, rap, sap, tap, chap, clap, flap, scrap, slap, snap, strap, trap, wrap, gag, lag, nag, sag, brag, drag, snag, stag, shag*

SORT 9   *OP, OT,* AND *OG* FAMILIES WITH WORDS AND PICTURES

(See page 24.) Introduce this sort in a manner similar to that described for Sort 7, except set up three headers. Sort pictures by rhyme and then add the words. The sort will look something like this:

op words and pictures		*ot* words and pictures		*og* words and pictures	
hop	mop	cot	hot	dog	jog
top	pop	dot	pot	log	frog

Additional Words.   bop, cop, sop, chop, crop, drop, flop, plop, prop, shop, slop, stop, got, jot, lot, not, rot, tot, blot, clot, plot, shot, slot, spot, trot, bog, cog, fog, hog, clog

SORT 10   *ET, EG,* AND *EN* FAMILIES WITH WORDS AND PICTURES

(See page 25.) Introduce this sort in a manner similar to Sort 7. The sort will look something like this:

et words and pictures		*eg* words and pictures		*en* words and pictures	
net	pet	beg	peg	hen	pen
jet	wet	leg		men	ten

Additional Words.   bet, get, let, met, set, vet, fret, Meg, Greg, Ben, den, when, then

SORT 11   *UG, UT,* AND *UN* FAMILIES WITH WORDS AND PICTURES

(See page 26.) Introduce this sort in a manner similar to Sort 7.

ug words and pictures		*ut* words and pictures		*un* words and pictures	
bug	tug	bun		cut	shut
jug	rug	run		hut	
mug		sun		nut	

Additional Words.   dug, hug, lug, pug, drug, plug, slug, chug, smug, snug, shrug, fun, gun, pun, spun, stun, but, gut, jut, rut, strut

SORT 12   IP, IG, AND ILL FAMILIES WITH WORDS AND PICTURES

(See page 27.) Introduce the sort in a manner similar to Sort 7.

ip words and pictures	ig words and pictures	ill words and pictures
lip	dig	hill
zip	pig	mill
rip	wig	pill

Additional Words.   *dip, hip, nip, sip, chip, clip, drip, flip, grip, ship, skip, slip, snip, strip, trip, whip, big, fig, gig, jig, rig, twig, bill, dill, fill, gill, ill, Jill, kill, quill, sill, till, will, chill, drill, frill, grill, skill, spill, still, thrill*

SPELL CHECK 2   ASSESSMENT FOR SAME-VOWEL WORD FAMILIES

(See page 28.) The word families studied up to this point are assessed with the Spell Check 2 for same-vowel word families. Recognition rather than production is assessed at this point, as students have not yet contrasted short vowels. Name each picture and ask students to circle the word that goes with the picture.

1. fan	**2.** hat	**3.** sad
4. map	**5.** log	**6.** top
7. jet	**8.** tag	**9.** cut
10. rug	**11.** bun	**12.** hill
13. dig	**14.** rip	**15.** dot

SORT 6   *at* **Family with Words and Pictures**

cat	mat	hat
rat	bat	fat
sat	pat	bat

SORT 7   *an* and *ad* Families with Words and Pictures

fan	dad	pan
sad	man	pad
van	mad	can

SORT 8 *ap* and *ag* **Families with Words and Pictures**

nap	wag	cap
rag	map	bag
tag	flag	lap

SORT 9   *op*, *ot*, and *og* Families with Words and Pictures

pot	dog	cot	hop
log	frog	top	jog
mop	dot	hot	pop

SORT 10   *et, eg,* and *en* Families with Words and Pictures

net	peg	jet	hen
pen	pet	beg	wet
leg	ten	men	

SORT 11   *ug*, *ut*, and *un* Families with Words and Pictures

run	cut	mug	jug
tug	sun	hut	rug
nut	bun	shut	bug

SORT 12   *ip, ig,* and *ill* **Families with Words and Pictures**

pig	pill	wig
lip	mill	hill
dig	zip	rip

Spell Check 2   Assessment for Same-Vowel Word Families
Circle the correct word.

Name _____

1 fat fan pan	**2** had hot hat	**3** sad sat mad
4 map mat mad	**5** lad log dog	**6** tap pot top
7 jet wet jog	**8** top tag rag	**9** not cat cut
10 rat rug bug	**11** bat run bun	**12** hill hit pill
13 dog dig dad	**14** rat rip rug	**15** top dog dot

Unit III Digraphs and Blends Picture Sorts

NOTES FOR THE TEACHER

Background and Objectives

Digraphs and blends consist of usually two and sometimes three consonants and may be referred to as consonant clusters. The consonants in **blends** retain their identity but are tightly meshed with each other as in the *st* of *step*. **Digraphs,** however, are two letters that represent only one unique sound—there is no blend involved. We generally recommend teaching the term *blend* but not the term *digraph,* because blend describes what is happening in a concrete way, but digraph does not. Students will:

- Sort pictures by beginning blends and digraphs
- Learn to segment and spell both consonant sounds in a blend
- Learn to spell the two letters associated with the single sound in digraphs *ch, sh, th,* and *wh*

Targeted Learners

These sorts can be used with middle letter name spellers who have mastered single consonants in the initial and final positions. Typically these children are in late kindergarten and early first grade. They may spell a few blends or digraphs correctly on a spelling inventory. Because these sorts involve only pictures, they can be used before students have an extensive sight vocabulary of words containing blends and digraphs. The Spell Checks on pages 42 and 52 can be used as pretests to determine your students' needs in this area. Some students are better at digraphs than blends and vice versa, whereas other students make mistakes with both. A spelling inventory or spell check can help you identify who needs these sorts.

Teaching Tips

Digraphs are presented first in five sorts. The first three sorts contrast *ch* and *sh* with *h* because that is often the confusion children show in their writing (e.g., *chip* may be spelled HP). All the digraphs are reviewed in Sort 17 and you may skip Sorts 13 to 16 if you think your students only need a review. Blends are covered in nine sorts. If your students seem to be catching on quickly, and this is likely to happen after you have worked with blends for several weeks, speed up your pace and do a new sort every few days. A slower pace would involve more steps that contrast single consonants with blends. For example, Sort 23 could be expanded to contrast *c, r,* and *cr*; *c, l,* and *cl*; *f, r,* and *fr*; and *f, l,* and *fl*. In Sort 24 you might contrast *b, l, r, bl,* and *br*. There are some additional pictures for such sorts in the Appendix of *WTW* if you want to create a handout or you may just want to model these expanded sorts with the group.

Some of the digraph sounds and letter combinations may not exist in other languages. For example, *sh*, *th*, and *wh* do not occur in Spanish and *ch* may be confused with *sh*. For English Language Learners, the sorts that contrast a single consonant such as *s* and *sh* are helpful and you may want to create a *t* and *th* contrast sort (do not expect students to sort by *w* and *wh*, however). Blends are also much less common in other languages. S-blends (*sl*, *st*, *sp*, etc.) do not exist in Spanish where the letter *e* precedes the two consonants as in *Éspanole*. You can expect that learning to say and hear the sound differences will require extra practice. It will be important to help ELLs name the pictures before sorting, during sorting, and after sorting. If students seem overwhelmed with too many new words, you may want to eliminate some pictures to reduce the number. *Words Their Way for English Language Learners* offers more information and ideas for alternative sorts.

Literature Connection

When possible, share books that contain a number of words with the targeted feature. For example, *Sheep in a Shop* (by Margot Apple) is a natural connection with the /sh/ sound.

Standard Routines for Use with Blends and Digraphs

1. *Repeated Work with the Pictures.*   Students should work with the featured sorts several times after the sort has been modeled and discussed with the teacher. After cutting out the pictures and using them for individual practice, students can store the pieces in an envelope or plastic bag to sort again several times on other days.

2. *Word Building, Blending, and Extending.*   If students have worked with the word families in Sorts 1 to 7 they will be familiar with building and blending activities. Although these sorts feature pictures and not words, each lesson will suggest possible words students can build or blend *while reviewing the families introduced previously.* For example, in the first lesson on *sh*, the words *shop*, *shot*, *shag*, *ship*, and *shut* can be used. Prepare a set of large cards on which you write the onset *sh* and then the rimes needed to make each word (*op*, *ot*, *ag*, *ip*, *ut*) or make copies from the back of this book. You can also do this with magnetic letters but keep the digraph or blend unit and rime unit together so that there are only two parts to blend into a word. For **building,** say the word and then model how to make the word by putting together the onset and then the rime. Children can then come up to make words or work with similar materials at their places (see the Appendix for letter cards). For **blending,** point to the onset and then the rime saying the sounds as slowly as possible without distortion (e.g., /shshshsh/ pause /oooop/), pointing to the *sh* and then the *op* as units. Then say the word naturally as you run your hand under it: *shop*. Model how you can change the rime to create a new word: *sh-ot*, *sh-ip*, *sh-ut*. Have the students say the sounds with you and then individually. For **extending,** these exercises will review word families (studied earlier) and demonstrate how those families plus knowledge of digraphs and blends can help students figure out many additional words. Keep the building and blending fast paced and use your own judgment about what words to use. *Shag* may be listed as a possible word, but it may make no sense to your students unless you can put it in a meaningful context.

3. *Draw and Label and Cut and Paste.* For seat work, students can draw and label pictures of things that begin with the target sounds/letters. They can also look for pictures of things and paste those into categories. The pictures from the cut-up sort can be pasted into columns and children should label the pictures. Do not expect accurate spelling of the vowels at this time.

4. *Word Hunts and Word Banks.* Students can look through their reading materials and word banks for words that have the targeted blends and digraphs.

5. *Reading.* Look for little books that have a number of words with the featured digraphs and blends. Be sure students can read these books with 90% accuracy on a second reading.

6. *Games and Other Activities.* The Show Me game described in Chapter 5 of *WTW* can be adapted for blends and digraphs and can be used for building words. Follow the Path games are described in Chapter 4 and can be adapted for beginning blends and digraphs. Shopping, Gruff Drops Troll at Bridge, and S-Blend Bingo can be downloaded from the CD-ROM.

SORT 13   *S, H,* AND *SH* DIGRAPH

Demonstrate, Sort, Check, and Reflect

(See page 37.)

1. Prepare a set of pictures to use for teacher-directed modeling. Use the letter cards as headers and display the pictures randomly. Begin the **sound sort** by modeling one word into each column explaining what you are doing: *Here is a picture of a hat.* Hat *starts like* hand *so I will put it under the letter* h. *This is a picture of a sheep.* Shshshshsheep *starts like* shoe *so I will put it under these two letters,* s-h. *Here is a sock.* Ssssock *starts with* s. *Now who can help me sort the rest of these pictures?* Continue with the children's help to sort all of the pictures, supplying the name of the picture as needed. Let mistakes go for now. When all the pictures have been sorted, name them in columns and check for any that need to be changed: *Do all of these sound alike at the beginning? Do we need to move any?*

2. Repeat the sort with the group, check by naming the picture in each column, and talk about how the words in each column are alike. You may want to point out that *sh* is special because it takes two letters to spell the sound.

s and sun	*h* and hand	*sh* and shoe	
saw	horse	shirt	shell
socks	house	ship	shop
soap	ham	sheep	shed/shack
seal	hose	shark	

Extend

Give each student a copy of the sort and assign them the task of cutting out the pictures and words to match them on their own in the same way they did in the group. On subsequent days students should repeat the sorting activity several times.

See the list of routines for follow-up activities to the basic sorting lesson. The words listed below are made up of rimes or word families studied earlier and can be used for building, blending, and extending or for the Show Me game.

Additional Words.   Words for building, blending, extending: *hip, sip, hop, hot, shot, hut, shut, shag*

SORT 14   *C, H,* AND *CH* DIGRAPH

(See page 38.) Introduce the sort in a manner similar to Sort 13. Sort twice with the group. Point out that *ch* is special because it takes two letters to spell the sound.

c and cat	h and hand	ch and chair	
comb	heart	cherry	chief
coat	hat	chimney	check
cake	horn	chin	chop
candy	hook	chick	

Additional Words.   *cat, chat, cap, chap, hip, chip, chill, hop, cop*

SORT 15   *H, SH,* AND *CH* DIGRAPHS

(See page 39.) This sort reviews *sh* and *ch* and may be optional. Introduce it in a manner similar to Sort 13. The sort will look something like this:

h and hand	sh and shoe		ch and chair	
hat	shed/shack	shower	cheese	chimney
hose	shop		chain	cherry
ham	sheep		chop	
house	shave		chief	

Additional Words.   See Sorts 13 and 14 for words with *sh* and *ch*.

SORT 16   *TH* AND *WH* DIGRAPHS

(See page 40.) Introduce the sort in a manner similar to Sort 13. Sort twice with the group. Again, you may want to point out that *wh* and *th* are special because it takes two letters to spell their sound.

Note: Children will confuse words that start with *w* and words that start with *wh,* so we do not recommend this as a picture sorting contrast because it is unlikely they can tell the difference in such words merely by sound.

th and thumb		wh and wheel	
thermos	thermometer	wheelbarrow	whale
thimble	thorn	whip	wheel
thirteen	think	whistle	wheat
thumb		whisker	whisk

Additional Words.   *that, than, then, when*

SORT 17   *SH, CH, TH,* AND *WH* DIGRAPHS

(See page 41.) Introduce the sort in a manner similar to Sort 13. Remind children that they have sorted these before and now they are combining all four.

shoe	chair	wheel	thumb
shelf	cheese	whisker	thorn
shot	chick	whistle	thimble
shark	chair	whip	thirteen
shave	chain	whale	thermos
shirt	chin	wheat	
ship			

Additional Words.   shop, shut, shag, chat, chap, chip, chill, chop, that, than, then, when

SPELL CHECK 3   ASSESSMENT FOR DIGRAPHS

(See page 42.) Assess students with Spell Check 3 for digraphs. Name each picture and ask students to spell the entire word. Only the beginning consonant or consonant digraph is counted right or wrong, but observe how much of the rest of the word students are able to spell. The pictures are:

1. chain
2. shark
3. sink
4. ship
5. two
6. whale
7. thumb
8. sheep
9. cheese
10. wheel
11. comb
12. thorn

SORT 18   *S, T,* AND *ST* BLEND

(See page 43.) Introduce the sort in a manner similar to Sort 13, but point out that the sound for *st* is called a *blend* because the two letters work together to make the sound. Model how these sounds can be segmented: /sssss/ + /t/.

s and sun	*t* and tent	*st* and star	
six	tie	stem	stick
sink	tire	stop	sting
scissors	top	stump	stir
		star	stool
		stamp	

Additional Words.   still, sun, stun

SORT 19   *SP, SK,* AND *SM* BLENDS

(See page 44.) Introduce the sort in a manner similar to Sort 13, but refer to the initial consonant pairs as *blends*. Talk about how these blends all begin with s so they need to pay special attention to the second letter. The sort will look something like this:

sp and spider		*sk* and skate		*sm* and smile
spool	sponge	ski	skip	smell
spoon		skull	skunk	smock
spear		skirt	skateboard	smoke
spill		skeleton		

Additional Words.   spot, spun, skill, smog

SORT 20   SC, SN, AND SW BLENDS

(See page 45.) Introduce the sort in a manner similar to Sort 13.

sc and scooter		*sn* and snail	*sw* and swing	
school	score	snake	swan	swim
scout	scale	snap	switch	
scarecrow		snowman	sweater	
scarf		snow	sweep	

Additional Words.   snip, snug, swig

Extend

Review all the s blends with games such as S-Blend Bingo on the CD-ROM.

SORT 21   P, L, AND PL BLEND

(See page 46.) Introduce the sort in a manner similar to Sort 13. This sort may be skipped if you want a faster pace. *Pl* is covered in Sort 22.

p and pig	*l* and lamp	*pl* and plus	
pail	lock	plug	plate
pin	log	plum	plane
pie	leaf	plant	plus
pan	letter	pliers	

Additional Words.   plan, lot, plot, lug, plop

SORT 22   PL, SL, AND BL BLENDS

(See page 47.) Introduce the sort in a manner similar to Sort 13.

sl and slide		*bl* and block		*pl* and plus	
sled	sleep	blindfold	blouse	plug	plate
sleeve	slide	block	blanket	plum	plane
slipper		blade		pliers	

Additional Words.   plan, plot, plop, blot, slap, slip, slot, slog, slug

SORT 23   CR, CL, FL, AND FR BLENDS

(See page 48.) Introduce the sort in a manner similar to Sort 13.

cr and crab	cl and cloud	fr and frog	fl and flag
crown	clip	fry	flower
crayon	clown	fruit	float
crib	clock	frame	fly
cry	clap	freckle	flashlight
crack	climb	freezer	
crackers			

Additional Words.   *crop, clan, clap, clot, frill, frog, fret, flap, flag, flip, flop*

SORT 24   BL, BR, GR, AND GL BLENDS

(See page 49.) Introduce the sort in a manner similar to Sort 13. *Bl* words are reviewed.

br and broom	bl and block	gr and grapes	gl and glasses
bride	blanket	grass	globe
bridge	blade	groceries	glass
bricks	blouse	grill	glue
bread	block	grapes	glove
brush	blow	grasshopper	
	blindfold		

Additional Words.   *brat, bran, Brad, brag, grip, glad, blot*

Extend

Review all the *l*-blends using pictures from Sorts 22, 23, and 24.

SORT 25   PR, TR, AND DR BLENDS

(See page 50.) Introduce the sort in a manner similar to Sort 13.

pr and present		dr and drum		tr and tree	
price	pretzel	drill	dream	trap	triangle
pray		dress	dragon	tracks	truck
prize		drip	drive	tractor	

Additional Words.   *trip, trot, drag, drop, drug*

Extend

Review all the *r*-blends with pictures (Sorts 23, 24, and 25) and games such as Gruff Drops Troll at the Bridge on the CD-ROM.

SORT 26   K, WH, QU, AND TW

(See page 51.) Introduce the sort in a manner similar to Sort 13. Note that this sort reviews the digraph *wh* and contrasts it with two blends that have the /w/ sound as part of them: *qu* and *tw*. *K* also contrasts with *qu*.

wh and wheel	*qu* and quilt	*tw* and twins	*k* and key
whip	quack	twelve	king
whistle	quarter	twist	kite
whale	queen	twenty	kick
whisker	question	tweezers	kitten
whisper	quiet		
wheat			
wheelbarrow			

Additional Words.   *when, quit, twig*

SPELL CHECK 4   ASSESSMENT FOR BLENDS

(See page 52.) Assess students with Spell Check 4 for blends. Name each picture and ask students to spell the entire word. Only the beginning blend is counted right or wrong, but observe how much of the rest of the word students are able to spell. The pictures are:

1. stem	2. flag	3. smile	4. drum
5. frame	6. grass	7. snail	8. plate
9. queen	10. swim	11. clap	12. tree
13. globe	14. twins	15. sled	16. brush
17. cry	18. price	19. spill	20. skate

SORT 13   *s, h,* and *sh* Digraph

s	h	sh

SORT 14   *c*, *h*, and *ch* Digraph

c	h	ch

SORT 15   *h, sh,* and *ch* Digraphs

h	sh	ch

SORT 16   *th* and *wh* Digraphs

SORT 17   *sh, ch, th,* and *wh* Digraphs

sh	ch	wh	th

Spell Check 3   Assessment for Digraphs

Name _____

1	2	3
4	5	6
7	8	9
10	11	12

SORT 18   *s, t,* and *st* Blend

SORT 19   *sp*, *sk*, and *sm* Blends

sp	sk	sm

SORT 20   *sc*, *sn*, and *sw* Blends

SC	sn	sw

SORT 21   *p, l,* and *pl* Blend

p	l	pl $2+1=3$

SORT 22   *pl, sl,* and *bl* Blends

sl	bl	pl 2+1=3

SORT 23 *cr, cl, fl,* and *fr* Blends

cr	cl	fr	fl

SORT 24   *bl, br, gr,* and *gl* Blends

br	bl	gr	gl

SORT 25 *pr, tr,* and *dr* Blends

pr	dr	tr

SORT 26 *k, wh, qu,* and *tw*

wh	qu	tw	k

Spell Check 4   Assessment for Blends

Name _____

1 ___	2 ___	3 ___	4 ___
5 ___	6 ___	7 ___	8 ___
9 ___	10 ___	11 ___	12 ___
13 ___	14 ___	15 ___	16 ___
17 ___	18 ___	19 ___	20 ___

Unit IV Mixed-Vowel Word Families

NOTES FOR THE TEACHER

Background and Objectives

In these word sorts different vowels will be compared in word families or phonograms to focus students' attention on the medial short-vowel sound. Students continue to practice blending skills as they mix and match onsets (including blends and digraphs) and rimes to figure out words. This reinforces the use of analogy as a decoding strategy. Students will:

- Sort words by rhyming sound and rime patterns
- Isolate, identify, and blend the onsets and rimes in word families
- Identify the medial short vowel in word families
- Read and spell the words in these sorts

Targeted Learners

These sorts can be used with middle letter name spellers who are using but confusing short medial vowels and representing consonant blends and digraphs in their spelling. Typically these children are in early to middle first grade and are beginning readers who are acquiring sight words at a good rate. Because theses sorts use words rather than pictures, it is important that students already know several of the words in each sort such as *cat* and *hat* in the *at* family or *hot* and *pot* in the *ot* family. Spell Check 5 on page 65 can be used to assess students further on word families.

Teaching Tips

There are seven sorts that use word families to contrast vowels. Most students will benefit from spending about a week with each of these sorts because there are more words in each sort and many will not be recognized immediately without repeated practice. Some different pacing scales and contrasts are suggested in *WTW*. There are many more word families that could be explored in similar sorts (see the Appendix of *WTW* for a list of word families), but by the middle of first grade most students can move on to other features once they have studied a sample of families. Now that students have studied blends and digraphs with pictures, be sure to include these features in building, blending, and extending. Look at the "Additional Words" after each sort for words to use for extending. Follow the same routines listed for same-vowel word families on pages 14–15 but consider the following additional routines.

> **Word Study Notebooks.** This is a good time to introduce words study notebooks described in Chapter 2 of *WTW*. Students can list the words from the sort, illustrate some of the words, and use words in sentences. They can also add more

words that come from word hunts or are introduced in building, blending, and extending activities.

Blind Sorts or No-Peeking Sorts. This is also a good time to introduce students to blind sorts or no-peeking sorts because they will find it easy to sort visually by the rime pattern. Model this activity first with the group and then let students work with partners under your supervision. After the headers are laid out, one student reads a word aloud to a partner without showing it. The other student indicates the category based on sound alone and points to the header. The word is then laid down immediately to check for accuracy. Students can also do a blind writing sort. As their partner calls a word without showing it, they must write it under the correct header.

The vowel system in English is much more complex than most other languages, so students learning English will struggle to pronounce new vowel sounds at the same time they are learning to identify them. It may be helpful for ELLs to continue to have the support of pictures as they study mixed-vowel word families and they might work with fewer words at a time. For example, you might create a sort contrasting the *at*, *ot*, and *ut* families using pictures and words from Sorts 6 to 12 and the blank template in the Appendix.

Literature Connection

When possible, share books that contain a number of words from the target families as a way to introduce or reinforce the families. See notes on page 14 in the unit on same-vowel word families. Some additional nursery rhymes have families introduced in these sorts.

- Hickory Dickory Dock: *ock* (*dock, clock*) and Wee Willie Winkie: *ock* (*lock, clock*)
  Humpty Dumpty: *all* (*wall, fall*)
  Jack Be Nimble: *ick* (*quick, stick*)
  Peter Peter Pumpkin Eater: *ell* (*shell, well*)
  Knick, Knack, Paddy Whack: *ack* (*knick, knack, whack*)

SORT 27   *AT, OT,* AND *IT* WORD FAMILIES

Demonstrate, Sort, Check, and Reflect

(See page 58.)

1. Introduce the words with a **visual sort;** that is, sort first and THEN read the words. Introduce the labeled pictures as headers. Explain that the students need to find more words for each word family. Model a word like *not*. Place it under *hot* and then read the header *hot* and then the word under it saying: Hot, not, *these words go in the same family because they rhyme.* Model several other words, and each time **sort the word first and then read** any accumulated words down from the header. Do not expect students to read the word first and then sort. They will be more successful at blending if they can use the header as a key word and then blend the new onset with the rime. As each word is sorted have the students join in as you read them from top to bottom.

2. After sorting all the words, ask the students how the words in each column are alike. Children should note that they rhyme and they are in the same family. Be sure to discuss how they all end with a *t* but have different vowels in the middle.

Explain that they will need to listen carefully to the vowel sound in order to sort the words.

3. Discuss the meanings of the words, especially those like *bat* that mean more than one thing.

cat		hot		sit	
bat	pat	not	lot	fit	lit
hat	rat	cot	pot	bit	pit
fat	sat	dot	rot	hit	
mat	that	got		kit	

4. Remove the words under each header and let the students repeat the sort together. Again, read all the words down from the top after sorting to check and encourage students to use the header and accumulating words to support their reading of unfamiliar words. This is very important because students are not likely to know how to read all the words in the family without some practice. Once more ask how the words are alike.

Extend

Give each student a copy of the sort to cut apart and use several times, and select from the list of standard routines. Introduce blind sorts or no-peeking sorts by modeling this in a group sort after students have had some practice sorting visually. Put up the headers and then read a word without showing it. Tell the students to listen carefully to the vowel: *The word is cot, Does cot go with* ca-a-a-t, h-o-o-t, *or* s-i-i-t? *Cot and hot are in the same family and both have the /ah/ sound in the middle.*

Additional Words.   *brat, chat, flat, scat, jot, plot, shot, spot, trot, quit, grit, skit, slit, spit*

SORT 28   *AN, UN,* AND *IN* WORD FAMILIES

(See page 59.) Introduce the sort in a manner similar to Sort 27.

can		pin		sun
fan	van	fin	grin	run
man	pan	win	skin	fun
tan	plan	chin		bun
ran	than	thin		

Additional Words.   *an, ban, Dan, clan, scan, bin, tin, shin, spin, gun, pun, spun*

SORT 29   *AD, ED, AB,* AND *OB* WORD FAMILIES

(See page 60.) Introduce the words with a **visual sort** as described in Sort 27 and repeat the sort together. Remember, sort first and then read all the words down from the top after sorting to encourage students to use the header and accumulating words to support their reading of unfamiliar words. Remember to discuss the meanings of such words as *tab* or *blob*. Introduce blind writing sorts.

sad		bed		crab		cob	
mad	pad	red	shed	tab	cab	rob	job
had	glad	fed	sled	lab		mob	blob
bad		led		grab		sob	glob

Additional Words.   *dad, rad, lad, dab, jab, nab, blab, scab, stab, slab, wed, bled, fled, shred, gob, snob, knob*

SORT 30   *AG, EG, IG, OG*, AND *UG* WORD FAMILIES

(See page 61.) Introduce the sort in a manner similar to Sort 27.

tag	dog	pig	bug	leg
rag	fog	dig	hug	beg
wag	jog	big	rug	peg
flag	frog	wig	plug	
snag		fig	drug	
		twig	slug	

Additional Words.   *bag, sag, nag, hag, lag, brag, drag, shag, gig, jig, rig, Meg, Greg, bog, hog, log, clog, dug, lug, mug, pug, tug, chug, smug, snug, shrug*

SORT 31   *ILL, ELL*, AND *ALL* WORD FAMILIES

(See page 62.) Introduce the sort in a manner similar to Sort 27.

pill		bell		ball	
hill	chill	tell	smell	mall	small
bill	still	fell		fall	
fill	spill	sell		hall	
mill	drill	well		tall	
will		shell		call	

Additional Words.   *Bill, dill, Jill, kill, grill, thrill, skill, quill, cell, dell, jell, spell, swell, dwell, wall, stall*

SORT 32   *ICK, ACK, OCK*, AND *UCK* WORD FAMILIES

(See page 63.) Introduce the sort in a manner similar to Sort 27.

sack		chick		sock	duck
tack	snack	lick	kick	lock	luck
pack	black	sick	quick	rock	tuck
back	quack	tick		clock	truck
rack		pick		block	stuck

Extend

So many words can be formed with these -*ck* words that it is worthwhile to spend a little extra time and create lists of all the words students can build, brainstorm, or find in their reading materials. *Eck* words could be added too (*neck, peck, deck, check, speck, wreck*). See the *WTW* CD-ROM for flip books.

Additional Words.   *Jack, lack, Mack, crack, clack, slack, smack, shack, stack, nick, wick, brick, click, flick, thick, trick, stick, slick, buck, muck, puck, suck, cluck, pluck, shuck, cock, dock, mock, tock, flock, smock, shock, stock*

SORT 33   *ISH*, *ASH*, AND *USH* WORD FAMILIES

(See page 64.) Introduce the sort in a manner similar to Sort 27.

fish	trash		brush	
wish	cash	flash	hush	blush
dish	mash	crash	rush	flush
swish	rash	smash	mush	
	dash		crush	

Additional Words.   *bash, gash, hash, lash, clash, slash, gush, lush, plush*

SPELL CHECK 5   ASSESSMENT FOR WORD FAMILIES WITH MIXED VOWELS

(See page 65.) Word families are assessed with Spell Check 5, which follows the collection of sorts. Name each picture and ask students to spell the word that goes with the picture. Students may not be able to complete this independently because of words such as *cash* and *sob*. Students should be able to spell the entire word correctly at this point!

1. pot
2. fin
3. sob
4. bun
5. mat
6. pan
7. rug
8. frog
9. beg
10. fall
11. hill
12. block
13. sled
14. tack
15. dish

SORT 27   *at*, *ot*, and *it* Word Families

cat	hot	sit
not	fit	hat
bat	cot	dot
got	fat	bit
hit	mat	lot
pot	kit	pat
rat	lit	rot
pit	sat	that

SORT 28   *an, un,* and *in* **Word Families**

can	pin	sun
run	fan	tan
man	bun	fun
fin	ran	van
pan	win	plan
chin	grin	than
skin	thin	

SORT 29   *ad, ed, ab*, and *ob* Word Families

sad	bed	crab
cob	job	mad
red	rob	lab
had	fed	mob
sob	bad	led
pad	tab	blob
grab	shed	glad
glob	cab	sled

SORT 30   *ag, eg, ig, og,* and *ug* Word Families

tag	dog	pig
bug	leg	hug
fog	dig	rag
beg	rug	big
wag	peg	wig
fig	jog	slug
flag	twig	plug
frog	drug	snag

SORT 31   *ill, ell, and all* Word Families

pill	bell	ball
fell	hill	tell
mall	bill	sell
fill	fall	hall
mill	call	will
tall	well	chill
smell	shell	still
spill	small	drill

SORT 32   *ick, ack, ock,* and *uck* Word Families

sack	chick	sock	duck
tack	lick		kick
luck	rock		pick
tuck	back		pack
lock	quick		tick
stuck	rack		block
truck	clock		snack
black	quack		sick

SORT 33 *ish, ash,* and *ush* Word Families

fish	trash	brush
cash	rush	mash
dish	hush	dash
rash	wish	mush
flash	crush	blush
swish	crash	flush
smash		

Spell Check 5   Assessment for Word Families with Mixed Vowels

Name _____

1 _____	2 _____	3 _____
4 _____	5 _____	6 _____
7 _____	8 _____	9 _____
10 _____	11 _____	12 _____
13 _____	14 _____	15 _____

Unit V   Picture Sorts for Short Vowels

NOTES FOR THE TEACHER

In these four optional sorts, different vowels will be compared using pictures to focus students' attention to the sound of the short vowels. In earlier sorts, students have had the support of word families and the printed word to make decisions about the medial vowel. With pictures, that support is removed and they must attend carefully to the sound only. These sorts can be used with students who know beginning and ending consonants but are using but confusing medial vowels. Typically these children are in early to middle first grade. You may find that these sorts are not necessary for all children. You can use Spell Check 6 page 74 to assess how well students can identify medial short vowels.

There are four sorts that use pictures to contrast vowels. You could spend about 3 to 5 days on each sort but you can also use these during the same time you use word Sorts 38 to 40 and alternate between using pictures and words. Additional sorts are on the *WTW* CD-ROM using different combinations of vowels.

These black line masters might be used for assessment purposes by asking students to spell the pictured word or just the vowel in the space beside the picture.

SORT 34   SHORT *A* AND *O* PICTURES

Demonstrate, Sort, Check, and Reflect

(See page 70.)

1. Make a set of pictures to use for teacher-directed modeling in a sound sort. Use *cat* and *sock* as headers and display the pictures randomly. Begin the sort by modeling one word into each column explaining what you are doing: *Here is a picture of a flag*. Flaaaaag *has the same vowel sound in the middle as* caaaat, *so I will put it under the* cat. *This is a picture of a mop*. Mooooop *has the same vowel sound in the middle as* sooooock, *so I will put it under the* sock. Continue with the children's help to sort all of the pictures. Let mistakes go for now. When all the pictures have been sorted, name them in columns and check for any that need to be changed: *Do all of these have the same vowel sound in the middle? Do we need to move any?*
2. Repeat the sort with the group, check by naming the pictures in the column, and talk about how the words are alike. The sort will look something like this:

a and cat			o and sock	
flag	bag		lock	mop
sack	jack		top	box
clap	grass		pot	rock
cap	can		fox	

Extend

Give each student a copy of the sort and assign them the task of cutting out the pictures to sort as they did in the group. On subsequent days students should repeat the sorting activity.

Standard routines for picture sorts on page 3 can be used as follow-up activities to the basic sorting lesson. You might want to use the word Sort template in the back of this book and write in the names of the pictures. Students could then match words to pictures. Students should be able to spell many of these words completely.

SORT 35   SHORT *I* AND *U* PICTURES

(See page 71.) Introduce the sort in a manner similar to Sort 34. The sort will look something like this:

i and pig			u and cup	
zip	lid		bus	gum
hill	lip		sun	bug
fin	wig		trunk	plus
fish	bib		cut	

SORT 36   SHORT *E, I, O,* AND *U* PICTURES

(See page 72.) Introduce the sort in a manner similar to Sort 34.

e and bed	i and pig	o and sock	u and cup
desk	six	dot	duck
net	clip	hop	bug
vest	kick	lock	truck
leg	ship	shop	rug
sled	stick	clock	brush

SORT 37   INITIAL SHORT-VOWEL PICTURES

(See page 73.) Use the letters to set up headers. Because there are few pictures that begin with these short vowels, the ones included here are more unusual than pictures in other sorts and will need some explanation. For example, it is not likely students can identify the *otter* or the word *ick* just from the pictures. Name the pictures for the students in advance and continue to assist them in remembering what they are called. **Do not expect students to be able to spell these words.**

apple	egg	igloo	octopus	umbrella
astronaut	Eskimo	itch	otter	up
ax	Etch-a sketch©	in	ostrich	underwater
alligator	Ed	ill	ox	upside down
add		ick	olive	
ant				

Additional Words.   Look for children's names in your class that start with these same short-vowel sounds: *Abigail, Allison, Alice, Edward, Isabell, Oscar, Oliver,* and so on. Add their names and/or pictures to the sort of initial short vowels.

SPELL CHECK 6   ASSESSMENT FOR SHORT VOWELS

(See page 74.) A form is provided at the end of the short-vowel picture sorts to assess students as a pretest or posttest. Name the pictures and ask students to write in the missing vowel. Some of these words have appeared in the sorts in this unit but others are new and assess transfer.

1. cap	**2.** bus	**3.** fox
4. zip	**5.** bag	**6.** desk
7. bug	**8.** rock	**9.** fish
10. grass	**11.** jet	**12.** lip
13. web	**14.** nut	**15.** mop

SORT 34   Short *a* and *o* Pictures

a	o	

SORT 35   Short *i* and *u* Pictures

SORT 36   Short *e, i, o,* and *u* Pictures

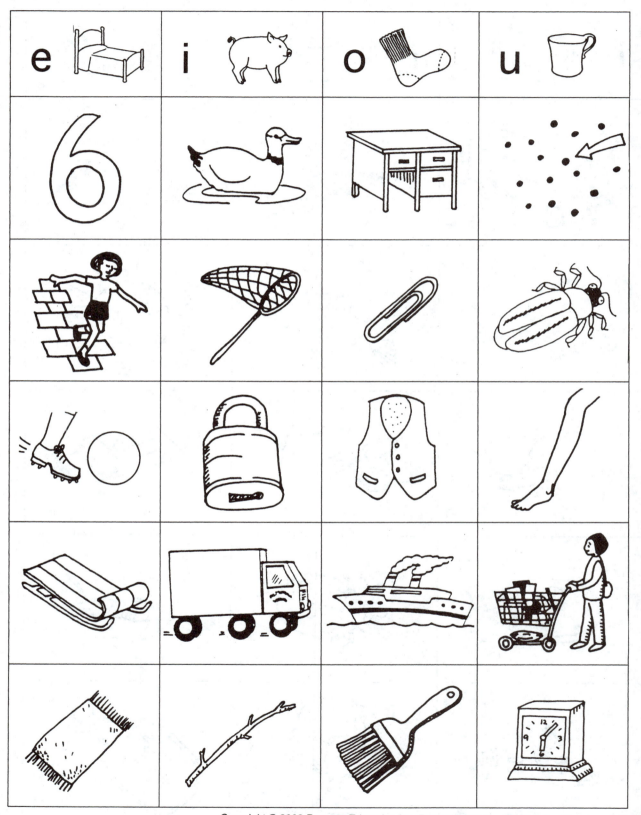

SORT 37   Initial Short-Vowel Pictures

Spell Check 6   Initial Short-Vowel Pictures
Write in the missing vowel.

Name _____

1 c — p	2 b — s	3 f — x
4 z — p	5 b — g	6 d — sk
7 b — g	8 r — ck	9 f — sh
10 gr — ss	11 j — t	12 l — p
13 w — b	14 n — t	15 m — p

Unit VI Short Vowels in CVC Words

NOTES FOR THE TEACHER

Background and Objectives

In these word sorts, different short vowels will be compared without the support of word families. Instead, students will learn to recognize the CVC pattern (consonant-vowel-consonant as in *bat* or *brat* or *blast*) in connection with the short-vowel sounds. In the next stage, within word pattern, this CVC pattern will be compared with long-vowel patterns. Students will:

- Segment all the sounds in a CVC word and identify the short-vowel sound
- Spell unit words with short vowels, blends, and digraphs correctly

Targeted Learners

These sorts are for students in the late letter name stage. On the primary spelling inventory, they should spell most blends and digraphs correctly and spell 5 to 6 short vowels correctly as well. Typically these children are in middle to late first grade and already should know how to read many CVC words. These sorts may also be used to review short vowels at the beginning of second grade, or with any students who need work on short vowels, blends, or digraphs. Spell check 7 found on page 94 can be used as a pretest or posttest for mastery. Short vowels are reviewed in the early within word pattern sorts, so if students miss only one or two short vowels and are using but confusing long-vowel markers that may be a better starting place.

Teaching Tips

It is important that students already know how to read most of the words in each sort, and many of the words studied earlier in word families will reappear here in the first few sorts. A number of high-frequency CVC words are included in these sorts and are marked with an asterisk. There may be some words students do not recognize at first and you must use your judgment about whether to keep those words in the sort (if there are only two or three this may be a good idea) or remove them, and/or substitute more familiar ones. Because there are 20 or so words in a sort some can be eliminated. Harder words are generally at the bottom of the word sort sheet. Expect that students who are familiar with sorting by families may be a little confused at first when they are asked to focus just on the vowel. Modeling the sort several times will help them learn where to direct their attention.

Oddballs are introduced and the first two sorts have a special header card to draw attention to the new category (later ones do not have this header but you can create one if you feel it is needed). There may be one or two words in a lesson that look like they have one of the featured sounds but do not.

There are 10 sorts that contrast short vowels. If you think students only need a review of short vowels before moving on to long vowels, then select the sorts that seem most appropriate and do not do all 10. If you think that your students need more practice with short vowels, there are additional words listed for each sort that can be written on the blank template at the end of the book.

English Language Learners may struggle to pronounce the short-vowel sounds correctly. Do not focus too much on correct pronunciation but give them many opportunities to say the words and pair them with native English speakers for cooperative sorting. You may want to reduce the number of words and pair words with pictures from sorts 34 to 37 to provide more support for learning the words. Take more time to discuss word meanings as you introduce each sort and continue to review meanings throughout the week. Asking students to illustrate some of the words as one of the weekly routines can reinforce the meanings as well.

Literature Connection

Use books for instruction that feature a number of CVC words so that children will see these words in the context of reading and have the opportunity to practice them. Many publishers are creating phonics readers or decodable text that can complement the study of short vowels but most books for beginning readers will have plenty of CVC words. Ideally you want to find books that students can read with 90% accuracy. Phyllis Trachtenburg created a list of trade books by phonics features that you can find online. Search by "Trachtenburg and trade books" or refer to the original article in *The Reading Teacher* (May 1990). The following books are good sources of CVC words with various short vowels.

The Cat in the Hat, Fox in Socks, and other easy readers (Dr. Seuss)
Who Took the Farmer's Hat? (Joan L. Nodset)
The Little Red Hen (Paul Galdone and others)
Titch (Pat Hutchins)

Standard Weekly Routines for Word Sorts

1. *Repeated Work with the Words.*   Students should work with the featured sorts several times after the sort has been modeled and discussed in the group. This is a good place to establish homework routines. See Chapter 3 of *WTW* for an example of a parent letter that you can send home to guide parents in reinforcing the classroom practice. See the Appendix for a worksheet that students can use independently at home.

2. *Writing Sorts and Word Study Notebooks.*   Students should record their word sorts by writing them into columns under the key words established in the group sort. Students may be asked to select some words to illustrate or to use some of them (not ALL of them) in sentences to demonstrate the meaning of the words.

3. *Blind Sorts or No-Peeking Sorts and Writing Sorts.*   With a partner (described in Chapter 3 of *WTW*) these are especially important so that students focus on sound as well as what they see in the printed word.

4. *Word Building, Blending, and Extending.*   Activities may now isolate the vowel to explore the CVC pattern in which there are three units to blend or spell as in *fl-a-sh*.

5. *Word Hunts.*   Look for words in daily reading materials that mirror the featured vowel sounds. Word hunts can extend children's understanding when they include

longer words such as *mitten* or *tablet* that have short-vowel sounds in two or more syllables.

6. *Games and Other Activities.*   The Show Me game is still a good activity for short vowels, but the focus may be more on changing vowel sounds than changing the onset as was done with word families. Look for other games in Chapter 5 of *WTW*. The Hopping Frog game is a favorite and can be downloaded from the CD-ROM. Slide a Word reviews preconsonantal nasals and final blends.

7. *Assessment.*   A weekly spelling test may become part of your routine by the late letter name stage. You may also want to select words from the additional word list for testing to see how well students can transfer their mastery of features.

SORT 38   SHORT *A* AND *O* IN EASY CVC WORDS

Demonstrate, Sort, Check, and Reflect

(See page 84.) Prepare a set of words to use for teacher-directed modeling. Many teachers make a transparency to cut apart and model sorting on the overhead projector. This sort might be used in connection with the short-vowel picture Sort 34. First sort the pictures to practice hearing the short-vowel sounds, then turn to the word sort. Later in the week students can glue down the picture sort and label the words.

1. Display the words and begin by asking the students to read over them to see if there are any they do not know or understand. Help them read and discuss the meaning of any that are unfamiliar.
2. Pull out the labeled headers *cat* and *sock*. Introduce the third header **"oddball."** Explain to the students that sometimes words do not have the sound we expect or do not have the same sound as the other words in the sort. In this sort there will be two oddballs.
3. Model a word such as *sad*. Place it under *cat*, reading the header and the word under it saying: Saaaad, caaaat—*these words have the same vowel sound in the middle.* (You can isolate the vowel by covering the letters in the word as you say *cat, at, a.*) Model several other words by reading the word and comparing it to the two headers. Include one of the two oddballs (*was, boy*) in your modeling, demonstrating how the word does not have either sound in the headers. Place it in the oddball category, leaving the other oddball for the students to discover.
4. Begin calling on students to decide where to place the other words. After sorting all the words, read them from the top and ask the students how the words in each column are alike. Introduce the term *short vowel* by saying something like: *These words have the short -a sound and these have the short -o sound.* Children should note that each column has the same vowel spelling and sound except for the oddballs. Point out that these words all have a similar pattern called CVC that stands for *consonant, vowel, consonant.* The sort will look something like this:

Short -*a* [cat]		Short -*o* [sock]		Oddball
sad	ham	box*	hop	was*
has*	had*	mom	lot	boy*
cab	wag	job	mop	
ran*	map	got*	top	
jam		fox	hot	

*High-frequency word

5. Because these words can simply be sorted visually by looking at the letters in the word, the second sort should be done by **sound.** Keep the same headers, but this time the teacher should say the word without showing it. Students take turns identifying where the word will go and can check as soon as the word is placed in the column.

Extend

Students should get their own words for sorts and engage in the routines suggested earlier. We especially encourage you to have your students work with a peer partner or a parent in a blind sort.

Additional Words.   dad, lad, van, fan, bag, sag, nag, lag, ram, yam, dam, lap, yap, jot, pot, mob, cob, cop, pop

SORT 39   SHORT *I* AND *U* IN EASY CVC WORDS

(See page 85.) Introduce the sort following similar steps as in Sort 38. Pictures for *i* and *u* are found in Sort 35. Model the oddball category again with the word *put*. Talk about the name of the sounds (short -*i* and short -*u*) as well as the CVC pattern in all the words.

Short -*i* [pig]		Short -*u* [cup]		Oddball
six	will*	but*	jug	put*
zip	him*	run*	tub	
rip	win	cut	fun	
bit	pin	nut	gum	
big*	did*	rub	hum	

*High-frequency word

Additional Words.   kit, lit, pit, fig, rig, bin, tin, bill, fill, pill, mill, hill, lid, rid, bud, hut, rut, hub, bum, pup

SORT 40   SHORT *E, I, O,* AND *U* IN EASY CVC WORDS

(See page 86.) Introduce the sort following similar steps as in Sort 38. Pictures are found in Sort 36. The word *get* may be an oddball depending on local dialect.

bed	pig	sock	cup	oddball
yes	six	not*	bus	saw*
let*	hid	pop	mud	her*
get*	mix	hot	cub	
tell*	his*		bug	
wet	miss		sun	

*High-frequency word

Additional Words.   (see lists above for *a, i, o, u*) bet, met, net, pet, set, vet, bed, fed, well, fell, sell, yell, bell, beg, peg, leg, hen, pen, men, den

SORT 41   SHORT A, I, E, WITH INITIAL DIGRAPHS

(See page 87.) Begin with an **open sort,** asking the students for their ideas about categories: *Who has an idea about how to sort these words? Is there another way?* These words should be sorted by the short-vowel sound but also by the beginning digraph; both of these should be modeled in the group. Reading these words may be challenging because of the initial digraph. Help students look at these words as onsets (in this case, a digraph) and rimes they may have seen in previous sorts (-*at,* -*ip,* -*in,* etc.). They still fit the CVC pattern because a digraph is a consonant unit. *What* is a high-frequency oddball in the short-vowel sort because it does not have a short -*a* sound.

Note that *th* has two slightly different sounds in these words. In *than* and *that* the sound is voiced, and in *thin* and *thick* the sound is unvoiced. This difference is felt in the vocal cords rather than in the mouth and is often completely overlooked by speakers of English.

Short vowel sort

that*	ship	when*	what*
chat	whip	check	
than*	chill	shed	
shall	this*	shell	
shack	which*	then*	
chap	chip	them*	
wham	chin		
	chick		
	thin		
	thick		

*High-frequency word

Digraph sort

ship	chip	whip	thin
shack	chat	wham	that
shall	chap	when	then
shed	check	which	them
shell	chill	what	thick
	chin		this
	chick		than

SORT 42   SHORT A AND I WITH INITIAL BLENDS

(See page 88.) Introduce the sort following similar steps as in Sort 41, sorting first by the short vowel. In addition, ask students if they can see other ways to sort the words. In this case the words can be sorted by whether the blend has an *l* or an *r* and this will leave *skip* and *spin* as oddballs that do not have either. These words are complex because of the initial blend. Help students look at these words as onsets (in this case a blend) and rimes they have seen in previous sorts (-*ad*, -*ag*, -*in*, etc.) as well as more examples of the CVC pattern. The short-vowel sort will look something like this:

glad	flat	cram	drip	grip
brag	plan	grab	flip	slip
flag	clap	crab	slid	grill
slap	trap	slam	clip	skip
brat	drag		drill	spin

The sort by blends will look something like this:

r-blend		*l*-blend		other
crab	trap	clip	plan	skip
cram	drill	clap	slam	spin
brag	drag	flag	slap	
brat	grab	flip	slip	
grill	grip	flat	slid	
drip		glad		

Additional Words.   *clan, snap, stab, slab, swam, gram, skit, spit, skill, spill, trip*

SORT 43   SHORT *E*, *O*, AND *U* WITH INITIAL BLENDS

(See page 89.) Begin with an **open sort,** asking the students for their ideas about categories. These words should be sorted by the short-vowel sound but can also be sorted by the kind of blend as in Sort 41. These words may be challenging because of the initial blends. There may be disagreement with some short vowels because of dialect differences. Some children may choose to put *cross, gloss,* and *frog* in the oddballs. *From* is an oddball for most of us.

Word sort by short vowel will look something like this:

trot	frog	sled	club	drug	from*
plot	slob	fret	glum	drum	
drop	gloss	dress	gruff	plum	
flop	slot	bled	slug	fluff	
cross			plug	truck	

*High-frequency word

r-blends and *l*-blends

cross	frog	bled	plug
dress	trot	club	plum
drop	truck	flop	sled
drum	gruff	fluff	slug
fret		glum	slob
drug		gloss	slot
from		plot	

Try combining all the words from Sort 42 as well as this sort to review the five short vowels and the *r* and *l* blends.

Additional Words. *blob, clod, glob, plop, crop, prop, spot, stop, sped, stem, step, spell, plus, scum, smug, snug, spun, stub*

SORT 44   SHORT VOWELS WITH FINAL BLENDS

(See page 90.) Begin with an open sort, asking the students for their ideas about categories. These words should be sorted by the short-vowel sound but can also be sorted by the final letter or final blend. As shown, *lt, lk,* and *lp* are grouped together. *Half* is an oddball because only the /f/ sound is heard and it is not a true blend.

Sort by short vowels

mask	desk	list	lost	just*
ask	best*	fist	soft	must*
fast	nest	gift	cost	tusk
raft	left*	milk		dust
last*	melt	lift		
half	help*			

*High-frequency word

Sort by final blend

mask	fast	raft	melt	half
ask	last	left	help	
desk	best	lift	milk	
tusk	list	gift		
	fist	soft		
	lost			
	cost			
	just			
	must			
	dust			
	nest			

Additional Words. *disk, husk, risk, task, bust, cast, past, mast, mist, self, pest, rest, test, vest, west, blast, chest, twist, trust, sift, swift, shift, craft, drift, felt, tilt, wilt, shelf*

SORT 45   SHORT VOWELS WITH FINAL DIGRAPHS

(See page 91.) Begin with an open sort, asking the students for their ideas about categories. These words should be sorted by the short-vowel sound and the final two letters in the word. *Push* and *wash* are oddballs in this sort because they do not have the expected short-vowel sound. Note: *Moth, cloth, toss,* and *boss* may not have the short sound depending on the regional pronunciation (/mawth/ or /clawth/). Double *ss* is included even though it is not considered a digraph.

Sort by short vowels

cash	fresh	rich	moth	much*	wash
class	guess	kiss	toss	such*	push
grass		wish*	cloth	rush	
bath		miss	boss	brush	
pass		with*			
math					
path					

*High-frequency word

Sort by final digraph

cash	rich	bath	class
fresh	much	math	grass
wish	such	path	pass
wash		moth	guess
rush		cloth	kiss
push		with	miss
brush			toss
			boss

Additional Words.   *dash, dish, hush, mash, mesh, rash, sash, blush, clash, crash, crush, flash, slush, smash, swish, trash, mass, bass, pass, brass, glass, mess, bless, hiss, loss*

SORT 46   SHORT VOWELS BEFORE *NG* AND *MP*

(See page 92.) Begin with an open sort, asking the students for their ideas about categories. These words can be sorted by the short-vowel sound but should also be sorted by the preconsonantal nasal at the end.

rang	bring	jump	stump
king	wing	camp	lump
long*	swing	bump	plump
sing	song	lamp	pump
rung	thing*	limp	ramp
sang	gang	stamp	
ring			

*High-frequency word

A building and blending lesson here might have students first make words such as *rag* and *ran*, and then change *ran* to *rang* to help them hear the subtle difference between those words. Words to contrast include: *rug/run/rung, sag/sang, rig/ring, wig/win/wing, hug/hung, cap/camp, plum/plump, lap/lamp, pup/pump,* and *rap/ram/ramp.*

Additional Words.   *bang, fang, hang, clang, slang, sling, cling, hung, sung, lung, bong, gong, tramp, damp, dump, champ, hump, rump, slump, thump*

SORT 47   SHORT VOWELS BEFORE *NT*, *ND*, AND *NK*

(See page 93.) Begin with an open sort, asking the students for their ideas about categories. These words can be sorted by the short-vowel sound but should also be sorted by the preconsonantal nasal at the end. *Want* is an oddball when you sort by vowels.

A building and blending lesson here might have students first make a word such as *hut* and then change it to *hunt* to help them hear the subtle difference between those words. Have students hold their nose as they say *hut* and *hunt* to feel the nasal sound in *hunt*. Words to contrast include: *wet/went, pat/pan/pant, had/hand, lad/land, win/wink, bun/bunk,* and *thin/think*.

went	print	hand*	stand*	junk	stink
hunt	plant	send	blend	pink	drink
ant	spent	land	and*	wink	thank
want*		wind		think*	blank
				bank	trunk

*High-frequency word

Additional Words.   *pant, chant, sand, band, grand, sank, spank, yank, drank, bunk, bent, dent, rent, tent, end, bend, mend, lend, spend, lint, link, sink, blink, bunt, runt, stunt, chunk*

SPELL CHECK 7   ASSESSMENT FOR SHORT VOWELS

(See page 94.) A form is provided at the end of the short-vowel sorts for students to use. Call the following words aloud for students to spell. Evaluate each word for the short vowel but note blends and digraphs as well. At this point students should be able to spell the entire word correctly.

1. bell	**2.** box	**3.** gum
4. chin	**5.** shed	**6.** mask
7. clock	**8.** truck	**9.** nest
10. fish	**11.** flag	**12.** drum
13. plant	**14.** hand	**15.** ring

SORT 38   Short *a* and *o* in Easy CVC Words

cat	sock	*oddball*
jam	sad	map
job	got	top
fox	hop	has
had	ran	box
wag	lot	mop
was	hot	boy
cab	mom	ham

SORT 39   Short *i* and *u* Vowels in Easy CVC Words

pig	cup	*oddball*
zip	bit	but
big	jug	pin
tub	rip	will
him	cut	rub
hum	win	fun
six	nut	run
put	did	gum

SORT 40   Short -e, -i, -o, and -u in Easy CVC Words

bed	pig	sock
cup	let	saw
hid	pop	not
her	mix	his
mud	six	yes
miss	cub	hot
wet	bus	tell
bug	get	sun

SORT 41 Short *a, i,* and *e* with Initial Digraphs

ship	chat	when
this	whip	shed
than	chip	chin
what	that	them
wham	then	thin
chill	check	which
shell	shack	shall
chick	chap	thick

SORT 42   Short *a* and *i* with Initial Blends

flag	slip	glad
clip	brag	flat
plan	drill	clap
grip	trap	grab
cram	drip	flip
crab	slid	drag
slam	slap	brat
grill	skip	spin

SORT 43   Short *e*, *o*, and *u* with Initial Blends

trot	club	sled
fret	plot	drop
glum	bled	flop
gruff	slug	plum
dress	cross	drum
plug	frog	drug
fluff	slob	truck
from	gloss	slot

SORT 44   Short Vowels with Final Blends

ask	gift	best
fast	desk	lost
must	last	just
cost	lift	melt
raft	help	fist
milk	soft	mask
tusk	nest	list
left	dust	half

SORT 45   Short Vowels with Final Digraphs

cash	rich	moth
class	path	boss
kiss	math	much
with	toss	wish
such	cloth	miss
rush	bath	pass
guess	fresh	grass
wash	brush	push

SORT 46   Short Vowels before *ng* and *mp*

rang	jump	king
camp	song	bump
sing	rung	lamp
limp	sang	ring
pump	gang	ramp
bring	wing	swing
stamp	long	stump
lump	thing	plump

SORT 47   **Short Vowels before *nt*, *nd*, and *nk***

went	hand	pink
send	wink	hunt
and	land	bank
ant	junk	wind
print	stink	plant
blank	spent	blend
stand	drink	thank
trunk	want	think

Spell Check 7   Assessment for Short Vowels

Name _____

1 _____	2 _____	3 _____
4 _____	5 _____	6 _____
7 _____	8 _____	9 _____
10 _____	11 _____	12 _____
13 _____	14 _____	15 _____

Unit VII Introduction to r-Influenced Vowels

NOTES FOR THE TEACHER
Background and Objectives

When *a* and *o* come before *r* as in *car* and *for* they do not have the same short sound as in *cat* and *hot* although they may sometimes be referred to as "short." These vowels have a unique sound and are known as **r-influenced** (or *r*-controlled). Because there are a good number of common words that contain these sounds, it makes sense to introduce them after the short vowels in their simplest forms. They will be revisited during the within word pattern stage in more complexity. In these sorts, *or* and *ar* will be compared to short-vowel words as a way to draw students' attention to the *r* as a letter that influences the vowel that comes before it. **Note** that after *w*, the vowel sound varies as in *word*, *work*, and *worm* and in *warm*, *warn*, and *war*. Some of these words will be included in these sorts as oddballs but they are not really irregular because they correspond to a small but fairly consistent category. Students will:

- Distinguish the sound between *r*-influenced short -*a* and -*o* and regular short -*a* and -*o*
- Read and spell the words in the unit correctly

Targeted Learners

These sorts can be used with students at the end of the letter name stage who have mastered short vowels as well as blends and digraphs. Typically these children are in late first grade. Spell Check 8 on page 100 can be used as a pretest and posttest.

Teaching Tips

Use the routines listed in the previous unit on pages 76–77. Because this is a new feature and offers some new challenges, plan to spend a week on each sort.

SORT 48   SHORT *O* AND *OR*

Demonstrate, Sort, Check, and Reflect

(See page 98.) Prepare a set of word cards to use for teacher-directed modeling.

1. Begin by asking the students to read over the words to see if there are any they do not know or understand. Ask what they notice about all the words. Probe until someone reports that they all have the letter *o*. Review with the students the sound

they learned in words such as *sock* and *hop*—what sound did the *o* represent? Ask i
all of these words have that sound.

2. Put out *sock* and *fork* as headers and read them, saying the words slowly to empha
size the sounds. Alert the students to watch out for three oddballs. Hold up a word
such as *corn*. Ask the students whether it should go under *fork* or *sock*. Continue with
student help until all words are sorted. *Word* and *work* are high-frequency oddballs
After saying each one slowly, help the children conclude that they do not go unde
either header because they do not have the right sounds and should be put in the
oddball category. *Your* can be sorted initially under *fork*.

3. After sorting all the words, read each column to verify that all the words have the
same sound. Ask how the words in each column look alike. (They all have the CVC
pattern but one column has only *or* and the sound is not short -*o*.) Talk about how
the final *r* changes the vowel sound that comes before it. Help students identify an
other oddball (*your*) that has the sound but a different pattern. The final sort wil
look something like this:

fork		sock		oddball
for*	torn	fox	pond	word*
corn	short	drop	spot	work*
fort	sport	rot	trot	your*
born	storm	shop		
sort	horn	rock		

*High-frequency word

Additional Words.   *cord, cork, form, thorn, pork, sword, snort, porch, north, horse, story
worm, worth, world*

Extend

Challenge Words.   Words that children can read and spell using familiar short-vowe
chunks include *morning, forgot, chorus, forest, hornet,* and *corncob.* You might childrer
to read or spell these two- and three-syllable words as a special challenge and introduc
tion to looking for familiar patterns in syllables.

SORT 49   SHORT *A* AND *AR*

(See page 99.) Introduce this sort in a manner similar to Sort 48. Some of the short -*a*
words have an *r*-blend in them to challenge students to think about where the *r* comes—
either before or after the vowel. *War* is an oddball in this sort. The high-frequency word
are may or may not be considered an oddball. The final sort will look something like this

star		cat	oddball
car	yard	brag	war
farm	shark	drag	are*
part	dark	crab	
far*	park	snap	
bark	jar	crash	
art	arm	trap	
card			

*High-frequency word

Additional Words.   *bar, cart, barn, dart, hard, harm, tart, yarn, charm, chart, scarf, scar, sharp, smart, march, large, charge, park, mark, spark, start*

Challenge Words.   *cargo, carpet, harvest, market, starfish, yardstick, barnyard, charming, garden, darkness*

SPELL CHECK 8   ASSESSMENT FOR R-INFLUENCED VOWELS

(See page 100.) Go over the names of the pictures and ask students to spell the word. They should be able to spell the entire word. The last three words are transfer words and were not included in the sorts.

1. corn	**2.** car	**3.** crab
4. shark	**5.** horn	**6.** fork
7. yard	**8.** shop	**9.** yarn
10. thorn	**11.** cork	**12.** card

Sort 48   Short *o* and *or*

sock	fork	*oddball*
fox	for	corn
fort	word	drop
rot	born	sort
your	shop	work
torn	short	pond
spot	sport	storm
trot	rock	horn

Sort 49   Short *a* and *ar*

cat 🐱	star ⭐	*oddball*
car	far	farm
drag	crab	jar
snap	bark	crash
art	war	card
trap	yard	are
dark	brag	shark
park	arm	part

Spell Check 8   Assessment for *r*-Influenced Vowels

Name _____

1 _____	2 _____	3 _____
4 _____	5 _____	6 _____
7 _____	8 _____	9 _____
10 _____	11 _____	12 _____

Unit VIII Contractions

NOTES FOR THE TEACHER

Contractions persist as a problem for spellers across a number of stages and you cannot expect mastery of them for some time. Some of the most frequent contractions are introduced in this sort in a simple manner and students can begin to understand how contractions are formed. We suggest teaching them at this point because students will be seeing them in their reading and using them in their writing. The words that make up these contractions have all been used in the sorts for late letter name–alphabetic spellers in this book. The placement of the apostrophe is not easy for young spellers to understand, but reading them seems to pose little trouble.

SORT 50 CONTRACTIONS

Demonstrate, Sort, Check, and Reflect

(See page 103.)

1. Prepare a set of word cards to use for teacher-directed modeling. Begin by holding up a contraction such as *I'm*. Select the card that contains the matching two words from which it was made: *I am*. Model a sentence for the students using both *I'm* and *I am*: *I'm your teacher* and *I am your teacher*. Repeat this with another pair such as *can't* and *can not*: *I can't go home yet* and *I can not go home yet*. Ask the students if both sentences mean the same thing. Ask them why they think we have two ways to say the same thing. Someone may suggest that *I'm* and *can't* are a shorter way of saying *I am* and *can not*. Continue to match each pair and ask students to provide sentences that use both. Ask the students if they see any way that the word pairs can be sorted. A final sort might look like this when sorted by the words that make up the contracted form:

I		is		not	
I'm	I am	it's	it is	can't	can not
I'll	I will	that's	that is	didn't	did not
		he's	he is	don't	do not
				wasn't	was not
				isn't	is not

2. Model how one or two letters are dropped in a contraction. Write *I am* and erase the a and replace it with an apostrophe. Repeat with several other words.
3. Repeat the sort with the students' help, check, and talk about what they have learned about contractions.

Extend

1. Students should get their own words to cut apart and sort for independent practice.
2. Word hunts will turn up other contractions (*what's, we're, haven't*, etc.) and students can be challenged to figure out what two words have been combined. Note that word hunts may also turn up possessive forms (*Pat's, Bill's*) so this may be a good time to briefly introduce that concept as well.
3. Writing sentences using both the contracted and noncontracted forms will help students understand the common meaning.
4. Concentation or Memory would be a good game to reinforce these pairs.
5. You can call these 10 contractions aloud for students to spell in order to check for mastery, but expect that they will continue to pose problems.

SORT 50   Contractions

I am	can not
can't	that's
it's	I'm
didn't	don't
do not	was not
I'll	he is
that is	did not
wasn't	I will
it is	is not
he's	isn't

Appendix

Letter Cards for Building, Blending, and Extending

Blank Template for Picture Sorts

Blank Template for Word Sorts

Independent Word Study Form

Word Sort Corpus

Letter Cards for Building, Blending, and Extending
1. Word Families with Pictures in Sorts 6–12

b	c	d	f	g	h
j	k	l	m	n	p
r	s	t	v	w	y
z	sh	fl	fr		
at	an	ad	ap	ag	ot
op	og	et	eg	en	un
ut	ug	ip	ig	ill	

Letter Cards for Building, Blending, and Extending
2. Digraphs and Blends for Sorts 13–26

sh	h	s	ch	c	th
wh	t	st	sp	sk	sc
sm	sn	p	l	pl	sl
sw	bl	cr	fr	cl	fl
bl	br	gl	gr	pr	tr
dr	k	qu	tw		

at	ot	it	an	un
in	ad	ed	ab	ob
ag	eg	ig	og	ug
ill	ell	all		ish

ick	uck	ock	ack
ash	ush	ish	

Letter Cards for Building, Blending, and Extending
4. Short Vowels and Final Clusters in Sorts 38–49

a	e	i	o	u	
b	c	d	f	g	h
j	k	l	m	n	p
r	s	t	v	w	x
y	z	sk	st	ft	lt
lk	sh	ch	th	ng	nt
nd	nk	mp		or	ar

Blank Template for Picture Sorts

Appendix

Blank Template for Word Sorts

Independent Word Study Form

1. Cut apart and sort your word cards first. Write a header or key word for each category, then write your words into columns below:

_____

_____

_____

_____

_____

_____

_____

_____

_____

_____

_____

_____

2. How are the words in each column alike? _____

_____

_____

_____

3. On the back of your paper write your headers or key words again. Mix up your words and ask someone to call them aloud as you write them under the correct header.

Word Sort Corpus: Number refers to the sort in which the word appears

Word	Sort	Word	Sort	Word	Sort	Word	Sort
and*	47	chick	32, 41	fit	27	hunt	47
ant	47	chill	31, 41	flag	8, 30, 42	hush	33
are*	49	chin	28, 41	flash	33	hut	11
arm	49	chip	41	flat	42	I'll	50
art	49	clap	42	flip	42	I'm	50
ask	44	class	45	flop	43	isn't	50
back*	32	clip	42	fluff	43	it's	50
bad	29	clock	32	flush	33	jam	38
bag	8	cloth	45	fog	30	jar	49
ball*	31	club	43	for*	48	jet	10
bank	47	cob	29	fork	48	job	29, 38
bark	49	corn	48	fort	48	jog	9, 30
bat	6, 27	cost	44	fox	38, 48	jug	11, 39
bath	45	cot	9, 27	fresh	45	jump	46
bed	29, 40	crab	29, 42, 49	fret	43	junk	47
beg	10, 30	cram	42	frog	9, 30, 43	just*	44
bell	31	crash	33, 49	from*	43	kick	32
best*	44	cross	43	fun	28, 39	king	46
big*	30, 39	crush	33	gang	46	kiss	45
bill	31	cub	40	get*	40	kit	27
bit	27, 39	cup	40	gift	44	lab	29
black*	32	cut	11, 39	glad	29, 42	lamp	46
blank	47	dad	7	glob	29	land	47
bled	43	dash	33	gloss	43	lap	8
blend	47	desk	44	glum	43	last*	44
blob	29	did*	39	got*	27, 38	led	29
block	32	didn't	50	grab	29, 42	left*	44
blush	33	dig	12, 30	grass	45	leg	10, 30
born	48	dish	33	grill	42	let*	40
boss	45	dog	9, 30	grin	28	lick	32
box*	38	don't	50	grip	42	lift	44
boy*	38	dot	9, 27	gruff	43	limp	46
brag	42, 49	drag	42, 49	guess	45	lip	12
brat	42	dress	43	gum	39	list	44
bring	46	drill	31, 42	had*	29, 38	lit	27
brush	33, 45	drink	47	half	44	lock	32
brush	45	drip	42	hall	31	log	9
bug	11, 30, 40	drop	43, 48	ham	38	long*	46
bump	46	drug	30, 43	hand*	47	lost	44
bun	11, 28	drum		has*	38	lot	27, 38
bus	40	duck	32	hat	6, 27	luck	32
but*	39	dust	44	he's	50	lump	46
cab	29, 38	fall	31	help	44	mad	7, 29
call*	31	fan	7, 28	hen	10	mall	31
camp	46	far*	49	her*	40	man*	7, 28
can*	7, 28	farm	49	hid	40	map	8, 38
can't	50	fast	44	hill	12, 31	mash	33
cap	8,	fat	6, 27	him*	39	mask	44
car	49	fed	29	his*	40	mat	6, 27
card	49	fell	31	hit	27	math	45
cash	33, 45	fig	30	hop	9, 38	melt	44
cat	6, 27, 49	fill	31	horn	48	men*	10
chap	41	fin	28	hot	9, 27, 38	milk	44
chat	41	fish	33	hug	30	mill	12, 31
check	41	fist	44	hum	39	miss	40, 45

*High-frequency words in Fry's top 200

Word	Page	Word	Page	Word	Page	Word	Page
mix	40	rag	8, 30	slot	43	thin	28, 41
mob	29	ramp	46	slug	30, 43	thing*	46
mom	38	ran*	28, 38	small	31	think*	47
mop	9, 38	rang	46	smash	33	this*	41
moth	45	rash	33	smell	31	tick	32
much*	45	rat	6, 27	snack	32	top	9, 38
mud	40	red*	29	snag	30	torn	48
mug	11	rich	45	snap	49	toss	45
mush	33	ring	46	sob	29	trap	42, 49
must*	44	rip	12, 39	sock	40, 48	trash	33
nap	8	rob	29	soft	44	trot	43, 48
nest	44	rock	32, 48	song	46	truck	32, 43
net	10	rot	27, 48	sort	48	trunk	47
not	*27, 40	rub	39	spent	47	tuck	32
nut	11, 39	rug	11, 30	spill	31	tug	11
pack	32	run*	11, 28, 39	spin	42	tusk	44
pad	7, 29	rung	46	sport	48	van	7, 28
pan	7, 28	rush	33, 45	spot	48	wag	8, 30, 38
part	49	sack	32	stamp	46	want*	47
pass	45	sad	7, 29, 38	stand*	47	was*	38
pat	6, 27	sang	46	star	49	wash	45
path	45	sat	6, 27	stick	32	wasn't	50
peg	10, 30	saw*	40	still	31	well	31
pet	10	self	44	stink	47	went	47
pick	32	sell	31	storm	48	wet	10, 40
pig	12, 30, 40	send	47	stuck	32	wham	41
pill	12, 31	shack	32, 41	stump	46	what*	41
pin	28, 39	shall*	41	such*	45	when*	41
pink	47	shark	49	sun	11	which*	41
pit	27	shed	29, 41	sun	28, 40	whip	41
plan	28, 42	shell	31, 41	swing	46	wig	12, 30
plant	47	ship	41	swish	33	will*	31, 39
plot	43	shop	48	tab	29	win	28, 39
plug	30, 43	short	48	tack	32	wind	47
plum	43	shut	11	tag	8, 30	wing	46
plump	46	sing	46	tall	31	wink	47
pond	48	sit	27	tan	28	wish*	33, 45
pop	9, 40	six	39	tell*	31, 40	with*	45
pot	9, 27	skin	28	ten	10, 40	word	48
print	47	skip	42	than*	28, 41	work*	48
pump	46	slam	42	thank	47	yard	49
push	45	slap	42	that*	27, 41	yes	40
put*	39	sled	29, 43	that's	50	your*	48
quack	32	slid	42	them*	41	zip	12, 39
rack	32	slip	42	then*	41		
raft	44	slob	43	thick	32		